Running a company is *that* simple...

W.P. Kromhout

September 2011

Production en publication by:
WPK Management Consulting BV
wpkromhout@gmail.com
September 2011

NUR: 801

Printing:
LULU

ISBN 978-1-257-95819-1

Table of contents

Part I.   Introduction and basic principles

1. Why read this book?

If you're hoping that this book will tell you what kind of business you should be in or what kind of product or service you should sell, I'm afraid you're going to be disappointed. This book is about neither of these. Nor is it about business models, markets and value chains.

This book is about how you should *organise* your business. It's about how you, as the director or managing board member, can make life a lot easier for yourself. How you can go home at a decent time of day without having to worry, and without losing sleep at night. It's about how you can make the best possible use of your staff to drive your business in the right direction and to make it as profitable as possible. It's about how to get the best out of your employees and how to select and retain them. It's also about making sure all your subordinates are all on the same wavelength, and how you can control what they're doing and how your business is developing in general.

In other words, this book is about how you run a business, irrespective of its nature and size. The principles set out here apply to just about any company. They can be used by the owner of two shops situated just one block away from each other, but even more by the CEO of a multinational with many operating companies in several continents across different time zones.

My aim is to demonstrate that all these companies can be run along the same lines. And I know that all company managers will benefit from reading it.

The book discusses concepts, structures and principles, illustrated by real-life examples from my career as a manager and CFO.

So why read *this* particular book?

Take a look around any bookshop in any airport. You'll find shelves and tables stacked with 'management books'. They're all about leadership, being effective, negotiating skills, organisational structures and so on. Twenty tips on how to get things done, 39 tips to do more with less: everything's there. However, I have yet to come across a concise and *simple* book about how to run a company. So here it is.

This book is also about how to keep things simple. Because that's how I like it. That's actually how most people like it. Simple is my favourite word. It's my middle name, if you like, because simple is effective.

That's also why I've tried to write to you directly, in plain English. I know that's how company directors like having things explained to them. Plain and simple, short and sharp. Solutions, not problems. Most managers already have far too much on their minds – and on their plates – as it is. If you want to dig really deep into one of the topics I touch upon, you'll have to find yourself a specialist publication on that particular subject. I have deliberately avoided going into too much detail in order to retain your attention.

This book contains practical approaches and concepts that you can start using tomorrow to help improve your business and turn it into an *excellent* company. Excellence in terms of control and 'manageability' is a foundation for commercial success. In Part III of this book, I will discuss a couple of individual issues that are particularly close to my heart. See them as extras, takeaways. They're part of the bargain.

If you apply the concepts, ideas and principles described in this book to your company, you'll hardly need a management development programme any more! Identifying and nurturing your top managers for the future will become part of the fabric of your organisation. And that's how it should be.

Yes, I do realise that life – and that means business, too – is often more complicated than is depicted in this book. I'm not naïve. I have lived through my share of difficulties in my business career. But I can say from my own experience: try to understand the basics as explained in this book. Let them sink in. Adopt them. You will find that they apply equally to more complex circumstances. Using them in such situations is the challenge you face.

This book is intended for business owners, investors, company directors, managers and anyone else who wishes to join their ranks and who is eager to run an excellent company.

I hope you find it interesting and useful reading.

2.   Basic principles and ground rules

Before you even start organising or reorganising your company, you have to agree on a set of basic principles and rules. Any community, whether it is a country, a family or a company, needs rules and governing principles. Since a company is not a democracy, the company directors and managers get to make up the rules.

Make sure the rules make sense, though. There's more chance of them being accepted by your staff if they do. If you communicate them properly too, you're off to a great start.

The other thing, of course, is to make sure you're fully aligned with your shareholders about especially the key principles. It's imperative that shareholders understand and endorse them. You're in for trouble down the road if you don't meet this condition.

Similarly, your fellow-directors must agree on the rules and principles before you start implementing them, otherwise they'll respond differently to the same day-to-day issues and will end up confusing the employees.

If you are thinking about taking on a position as a board member, make sure that the main points are on the table. Discuss them and establish whether your views are in line with those held by the rest of the board. If not, you may be climbing aboard the wrong boat.

Once the entire board is in full agreement on the principles and rules, you need to communicate them to everyone in the company. Don't underestimate the importance of this. A good communication plan is very useful here. Don't forget that most people actually like having rules to abide by. They give them something to hang on to.

'In my book', there are four *basic principles*:

1. Break up activities and make people accountable
2. Decentralise as much as you can
3. Allow your business units to choose their own suppliers, and
4. Keep things simple!

You'll notice that these basic principles have entirely different dimensions. This is quite deliberate. Don't worry, all will be made clear.

And here are my seven *ground rules for effective behaviour*. They are more like behavioural values. They are rules about how people should behave in a company in order to make it most effective. They're about how people should work with one another. If everyone in your operation sticks to them, you're already well underway to becoming a very good company:

1. Treat your colleagues like customers
2. A deadline is a deadline: stick to your promises
3. Base your decisions on facts and figures
4. Get it right first time
5. It's OK to make mistakes (as long as you learn from them)
6. Listen
7. Set a good example for others to follow

Apart from these principles and ground rules, companies will have many other – often far more detailed – rules. These are generally known as policies and procedures. A company's basic principles, ground rules and policies and procedures, together with its mission and vision statement, form the framework within which the company and its business units operate. This framework is 'owned' and maintained by headquarters (HQ). We'll come back to this later.

As I said, the above are *my* basic principles and ground rules. Don't just copy them blindly. Think about them. Let them sink in. Discuss them and amend them where you believe this is appropriate. You really need to buy into them, and *believe* in them if you want to successfully apply them. So read on.

3. The four basic principles

3.1 Break up activities and make people accountable

You have got to break up your company into smaller units headed by someone who, while acting within a basic framework, is responsible and accountable for that unit's *performance*. Whilst *financial* performance is probably the main measure here, it is not necessarily the sole measure. Performance comes in many shapes, depending on your activities and the stage of development your business has reached. Measuring your business units' performance should therefore also involve looking at non-financial qualitative and quantitative indicators, as long as they are measurable and objective. We'll return to this point later (in chapter 12).

If you don't make people responsible and accountable, or if you allow inconsistent behaviour among the managing board to undermine this principle, your company will become unmanageable and you, i.e. the directors, will end up not going home from work at a decent time. You'll be constantly caught out by surprises and will have loads to worry about.

It is not always clear how you should set about breaking up a company into logical and effective units; in many cases, it's a complex business. This book will help you make the right choices by providing practical guidelines.

3.2 Decentralise

Another important principle is that company directors and managers should not try and do things that other people can do better. This sounds like a no-brainer. But in fact, it touches the core of a recurring debate that crops up in just about every single company: the argument about the relative merits of centralisation and decentralisation. Decentralisation means no more than *structurally delegating responsibility* from headquarters to the business units. My principle is: don't centralise unless there are very good - compelling - reasons for doing so. Let the business units and their staff – who are closest to the problem affecting them – deal with it at first hand. They can do it quicker and more efficiently than you, simply thanks to the fact that they are *close* to it. If you made them responsible, you'll find that they often fix a problem even before you find out about it. If you ever do.

I will discuss centralisation and decentralisation later on, but please remember that this matter is absolutely critical. If you think that I'm an enemy of centralisation, you're absolutely right. I am. But if you think that means I don't believe in centralising anything at all, you're very wrong. There are often very good reasons for centralising certain aspects of a business (see further in chapter 5). However, the basic principle remains: don't do it, unless you have very good reasons for doing so.

3.3   Free choice of supplier

The third basic principle is giving people the *freedom to choose their own suppliers*. It may feel a bit out of place here (too detailed, too specific), but believe me: it is very basic and applies in many different situations. This principle is both consistent with the previous two and equally important.

If you make people responsible for part of your business, you've got to give them leeway. In other words, you should allow them to choose their own suppliers. All within the boundaries of company policies and procedures, of course.

It is simply wrong to force your business units to use an in-house supplier just because the latter happens to be part of the same group. If you do this, it's not good for the supplier as he will grow lazy and lose his competitive drive. Nor is it good for the unit, as the staff will get frustrated and demotivated by their inability to make their own decisions. Their reaction will even be more forceful if they don't get value for money either.

There's no objection to designating group companies as each other's preferred suppliers, or to giving them the right to match a third-party proposal. That's all just fine, but don't impose a closed shop on your units, i.e. an obligation to use internal suppliers. In the long run, it will prove highly detrimental to your business. I'll go into this in more detail in Chapter 14.

3.4   Keep things simple

Maybe I should have started with this one, because it's difficult to overrate its importance. It really is an overriding principle to which I constantly adhere: keep things simple.

Keeping things simple is all about ideas, structures, procedures, instructions, systems, communication – in fact, *everything* in business. If you make things complicated, they won't stick. They'll get 'lost in translation' and simply won't work. People already have far too much on their minds; they want things to be simple.

Look at politicians. Why do populists tend to win elections? Because they keep it simple. Their gift is an ability to translate ideas, controversial or not, into soundbites, one-liners. And it works.

You've got to do the same in managing a business. Whether you create a wonderful reporting system, a comprehensive application form or a scientifically tested method of evaluating business cases, you risk losing your audience. Most things don't have to be perfect to work. Good is good enough.

I'll give you some examples later on to show why even perfect is no good if it is not simple. You have to compromise in order to be *effective*. Simple is effective, effective is good. It's better to be 60% correct and effective than 100% correct but not effective at all.

You'll see later on how the term 'simple' can be applied to things like balanced business scorecards, economic value added (EVA), management accounting and group structures. As I said, if you don't keep things simple, people won't be able (or willing) to work with the tools you give them and they will therefore not be effective. In fact, you'll see that I apply *simple* to almost everything.

4. The seven ground rules for effective behaviour

In Chapter 2, I listed seven ground rules and explained that if the staff working for a company adhered to all of them, that company would be on its way to becoming a very good company. Here's how they work.

4.1 Treat your colleagues like customers

In many companies, staff treat their fellow-employees, especially if they're lower in rank, like third-class citizens. I've seen cases in which people only open emails from higher- ranking employees and ignore e-mails from their peers, let alone from lower-ranking colleagues. This is wrong. Remember:

- your colleague wants something from you so that they can do their job; they work for the same company;
- your colleague will give you a bad press if you don't treat him or her with respect. A bad reputation can easily undermine your effectiveness and may ultimately ruin your career;
- someone who is now your subordinate may later become a peer or perhaps even your boss;
- you may need your colleague next time;
- a company is a team; a team performs better than a bunch of individuals.

Let me give you a simple example of how you can treat your colleagues as 'customers'. In my company, expense claims from colleagues always end up at the top of the pile. They are handled and paid immediately. People who advance their own money for the company should get it back the same day if possible, with thanks.

Conversely, people are often highly annoyed if they don't get repaid quickly. Next time, they'll ask for an advance or a corporate credit card before spending money on the company's behalf. Or they'll simply decline to go the extra mile for their employer. This is behaviour that is easy to avoid.

4.2   A deadline is a deadline: stick to your promises

Many companies have a culture of imposing deadlines that have a degree of slack built in to them. This is wrong on two counts. First of all, you don't impose deadlines, you agree on them. If you want commitment and you want people to go the extra mile, you need them to commit to deadlines. Secondly, if you build in slack in a deadline – a practice for which people who impose deadlines are notorious – you can be assured of one thing: your deadline will not be met. The guy at the other end will know soon enough that you have built in slack, because you always do.

It's all easy enough. Just agree on a realistic deadline with the party who has to deliver the goods. If you take your subordinate seriously, he or she *will* deliver. If they don't, they have a problem. They will know it, too, because they will have broken a ground rule.

A culture of imposing deadlines and building in slack and no repercussions for late delivery will make it much less likely that you achieve your goal of becoming a good company.

4.3   Base your decisions on facts and figures

Take a look around and you'll see just how many decisions are based on hearsay, gossip, estimates or gut feeling. Again, the message is simple: know your facts and figures, and use them in taking decisions. It may take a bit longer, but it's better to be safe than sorry.

4.4   Get it right first time

It is amazing how many *unnecessary* mistakes businesses make. Order a new kitchen, or build an extension to your house and you'll see what I mean. It's true that you can't make an omelette without breaking eggs, but many mistakes are very easy to avoid. Not making mistakes saves time, money and irritation.

It's often just a matter of being more diligent, of taking a bit more time, putting in a bit more effort or simply helping one another and asking the right questions. Ask your people: WHY? Ask it again, and again, every time in a different way. If you get convincing, consistent answers every single time, you can be pretty sure your people know what they're doing. Sometimes it's just a matter of applying the previous ground rule: base your decisions on facts and figures.

Remember that the cost of correcting a mistake is always a multiple of getting it right first time around. Errors in service delivery can literally ruin a company. Even mistakes in internal processes can be extremely costly to remedy. In an accounts department, for example, the job of clearing backlogs, removing double entries and double payments, and dealing with un-reconciled sub-ledgers, intercompany discrepancies and open items sitting in suspense accounts is not one that can be done by your current financial staff. You'll need to buy in a lot of additional manpower (at a high cost) to solve these problems.

This is without mentioning the potential *indirect* cost of such errors. In this particular case, the indirect effect may be that you don't know your numbers. This is like driving a car in the dark without headlights: dangerous and potentially very costly.

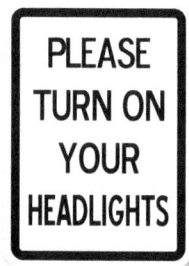

PLEASE TURN ON YOUR HEADLIGHTS

Indirect costs are often impossible to measure. Don't let it get to that point. Keep things under control and create capacity (in both qualitative and quantitative terms) before you actually need it.

Now that I mention it: people often forget to plan for holidays and sick leave. That's a guaranteed way of starting off on the wrong foot. While you're at it, plan for unexpected events as well as for regular staff absences. Don't be penny-wise and pound-foolish in sizing your staff complement.

4.5   It's OK to make mistakes

Although this appears at first sight to be inconsistent with the previous ground rule, it's not. As I said, people are bound to make mistakes from time to time. It's a fact of life. So let's agree that they should only make *necessary* mistakes.

Managers need to allow staff to make *necessary* mistakes. It's important to avoid an atmosphere of deceit, ducking and diving, and finger pointing, as this undermines staff morale and is therefore bad for business.

Moreover, if the company culture is right, people are much more likely to quickly report a problem and seek assistance. The longer an issue stays undetected, the greater the potential impact.

Avoiding surprises is key here. A mistake can be an inaccurate estimate or an unrealistic deadline for a delivery. These things can happen. If they do, your subordinate should see them coming, so instruct him not to wait until the deadline before telling you that he or she is not ready. Let him manage your expectations and give you an opportunity to intervene, to assist.

I've yet to come across someone who never makes a mistake. Some of the best managers I know have made big mistakes in the past. That's probably why they are so good today. A company and the people who work for it should learn from their mistakes. That's why I would even call these mistakes *necessary*. They're the ones you learn from, the ones that make you better.

4.6   Listen

In any human interaction, it is crucial that people *listen* to one another. Listening is much more than just hearing. It's all about hearing, understanding and thinking.

This applies just as much to an organisation. Company directors need to *listen* to other people, hear out their ideas and think about those ideas before making a decision. Also, make sure you air your *own* ideas, ask for feedback, think, decide and act. Don't see *listening* to subordinates as a weakness. It's the kind of behaviour that should become an integral part of your company culture. It's a way of stimulating and developing skills throughout the organisation.

4.7   Set a good example

This is my final ground rule. Directors need to set the right example. This is a particular powerful passion – some would say even an obsession – of mine. Whether we're talking about business ethics, expense claims, getting to meetings on time or keeping to working hours: your staff are watching you. And this one also applies to the other six ground rules: company directors need to set the example.

If a company adopts a policy of economy-class travel for all members of staff (which I would not recommend, by the way), board members should also fly economy class. If a company cuts bonuses, those paid to board members should also be affected. If the board members expect people to work long hours, they have to do the same. Conversely, if they want people to go home in time, they have to clock off on time themselves, too.

You cannot apply other rules to yourself than you impose on others. You cannot place yourself above the law. You'll lose support if you do. And if you lose support, you'll be less effective in your job.

Do bear in mind, though, that this is a 'Western' perspective. There are other cultures in which things are entirely different. In some countries, the opposite may even be true: directors *must* behave differently in certain respects, in order to enforce their status. I'll discuss this in more detail in Chapter 15, as this can be an important factor if you are running a business in a multinational (i.e. multicultural) setting.

Part II.   Structure, reporting and control

5.   Centralisation versus decentralisation

5.1   The management consultants' mantra?

The case of centralisation versus decentralisation is without doubt one of the classic issues of debate among management consultants and senior company managers. Many companies have gone through the pain of centralised restructuring. Others keep struggling with the problem, passing through the full cycle again and again in an attempt to find the right balance. Many companies never *find* the right balance.

Believe me, I have experienced my share of it too, having lived through a very strong centralisation being undertaken concurrently with the relocation of corporate headquarters from one side of a continent to the other.

The main pitfall with centralisation is that, on the drawing board, in spreadsheets and on PowerPoint slides, it always seems to make so much sense. It means big savings in overheads – on paper, at least. Creating competence centres and amalgamating support departments creates lots of synergy. In fact, it looks very much like a 'slam-dunk' decision. The economies of scale are simply waiting to be picked. Combining accounts departments from all over the world, merging HR departments, IT departments, business development staff, and putting them all in one location, one building all boosts overall efficiency. Or doesn't it?

Management consultants are only too happy to tell you to centralise. They will calculate the cost savings for you. And you can be confident they're going to be huge. Centralisation will also give you better control over your business. Controlling everything from one place, close to the managing board, must be better, right? In short, centralisation is one of the leading mantras of management consultancy.

What management consultants always forget to work out is the amount of time and money you lose on communication and coordination, and on the local advisors you need to engage to make up for the lack of local knowledge. Nor are they ever willing to acknowledge the devastating effect centralisation has on the morale of local staff.

5.2   The effect of centralisation on your local staff

If you force your local management to ask headquarters for permission to go ahead with every single decision, they'll lose interest and motivation and will eventually leave the company. Don't worry, though, they won't *all* leave. Only the good ones will, frustrated by the absence of career prospects.

But why don't these management consultants calculate these costs? Because it's impossible to do so. You wouldn't even know where to start. Besides, they will have moved on by the time you find out that something has gone wrong along the way. You won't be able to stick it on them anyway. They'll simply say that the centralisation exercise was not properly implemented.

What management consultants also forget to tell you is how much easier – and cheaper – it is to solve a problem at source and as soon as it occurs rather than from a distance, with an endless series of e-mails, memos and conference calls.

Do you actually know why so much went wrong locally to start with? Because the local managers no longer care. They're not empowered. They don't feel responsible and they're not motivated. The good ones left the company some time ago, remember? You chased them away. You're now trapped in a vicious circle.

Be aware that headquarters-bashing is a favourite hobby in any organisation. This is another truism. It applies at all times, whatever you do, and however good you are. *'It's HQ staff who wear the flashy suits, earn the big salaries and scratch each other's backs. They're the ones who aren't accountable and who live off the money made by the local business units. So if, on top of that, headquarters wants to take every single decision and have a say in every local issue, then they can have it. Then everything that goes wrong is by definition their fault too.'*

By centralising all decision-making, you are creating a breeding ground for these feelings. It's a recipe for disaster, a formula for failure caused by a company running out of control. Centralisation is a dead end.

5.3   The way forward

The above illustrates why the debate on centralisation and decentralisation is so incredibly important, and why it's so difficult to move from one model to the other. It takes courage to move from a centralised - yet failing - organisation to a more decentralised one. It means letting go. It obliges you to stop taking every single decision on behalf of your local operations. It's almost like seeing your children move out and become independent.

In other words, it means that you must trust your local management. In management consultancy terms, you need to *empower* them. You've got to give them the proper tools and, most importantly, you've got to put the right people in the right places. People with the right skill set and mentality. Err, yeah, right – these are the people who just left you. That's why you need guts to make this change. But you have to. There is no other way.

This is what makes this step so difficult. Every nerve in your body tells you to move forward with centralisation *'because the local staff are incompetent and making a mess of it. So many things are going wrong. Customers are dissatisfied and are taking their custom to our competitors. Spending is over budget and money is being wasted. All these local staff are idiots! HQ has to take even the most minor of decisions and interfere with everything. The locals can't get anything right.'*

The result is a bigger team of controllers, more e-mails, more reports, more conference calls, more travel, and more meetings with everyone at HQ. In fact, more of everything, until you suffocate.

You need to break this vicious circle of local failure and decision-making at headquarters. But where do you start?

It's simple. Make a leap of faith and start locally. Identify and recruit the right people with the proper mentality and skill set and tell them what your plans are. Tell them that you will train them, coach them and give them a proper framework including your values (i.e. the basic principles and ground rules for effective behaviour), and that you will empower them to work within this framework. They will pay you back. Trust them. What have you got to lose?

Secondly, get rid of all those know-alls at HQ, those people who think they can micro-manage the whole world from an ivory tower. How can anyone accept such a mission impossible in the first place? Retain only policy-makers - who understand your business - and people who have a vision of the future. Some of the better HQ staff may be interested into moving to a local operation. Some of them may actually get a kick out of *seeing* an operation for a change. If they don't, let them go.

6   The role of headquarters

6.1   The six-million dollar question

So what should you organise locally and what should you do at headquarters?

This is the six-million dollar question to which there is no set answer. Every organisation is different. The size, type of business, ownership structure, competition, locations, time zones, jurisdictions, cultures, markets and capital intensity (to name just some of the factors) all come into play in answering this question. However, there are a couple of important principles to consider.

Let's start off by saying that headquarters is only there to set the rules, to make sure everyone sticks to them, and to support the local operations. Another way of saying this is that headquarters should define the company's operating framework and make sure that the right conditions are in place for doing business. Everything headquarters does is related in one way or another to this.

In order to be able to create the right conditions, headquarters will also have to report on how things are going to the company's owners and financiers. If HQ doesn't, the funds will dry up very quickly. So that's something you need to organise, too. Headquarters also needs to formulate and implement a strategy and make sure the organisation acts as one. This implies a big coordinating role.

A corporate strategy could also include expansion – aimed at creating more economies of scale – by means of acquisitions. Identifying potential targets, undertaking due diligence investigations and closing deals are typical corporate tasks.

All good stuff, and more than a plateful for headquarters.

6.2   Setting the rules

Setting the rules can be a complex matter. You need experienced managers and policy-makers who are good communicators and understand the business to do that. If headquarters does not understand the business, it will introduce the 'wrong' rules and will then proceed to lose first support and ultimately control. To be 'right' (i.e. effective), the rules need to be easy to understand, practical and to the point.

These are the long-term, more structural, elements of the framework, which require regular maintenance and which must be designed and implemented by headquarters:
- mission statement and long-term vision
- basic principles and ground rules (for effective behaviour)
- policies and procedures

These are the variable elements of the framework, to be prepared periodically and mutually *agreed* by headquarters and the business units:
- annual plan and budget [1]
- medium-term outlook (3-5 years), to be updated every other year
- (a long-term outlook beyond 5 years, where relevant)

---

[1] The term 'budget' refers to an annual publication containing estimates of the targeted numbers, whereas the term 'annual plan' refers to the targeted annual *plans and/actions* that the organisation in question envisages for the coming year. These two ingredients are often combined into one a single document, which is commonly referred to as an 'annual plan'.

6.3   Mission statement & long-term vision

Many papers have already been written on mission[2] and vision statements and I'm not planning to reproduce or summarise them here.

Not all organisations have a vision and/or a mission statement and some very prominent organisations operate perfectly well without one. To be honest, I don't have strong feelings either way.

I do know though that describing your organisation's long-term *vision* and your more concrete *mission* in a powerful sentence or two can be a first step in aligning your staff. It can be an excellent way of kick-starting a new working method and it can be a useful tool to help companies that have gone astray to get back on track. Getting (senior) managers to think long and hard about their company's long-term vision and mission can be a very constructive process, especially where an organisation needs to get off to a fresh start.

Do make sure, though, that any statements you formulate are clear, meaningful and appealing. Don't turn them into gratuitous remarks, otherwise you might as well not bother.

It's for these reasons that I want to mention 'mission and vision' here. They can form a logical first component of the framework within which managers operate and which is so important for running a company.

---

[2] See www.missionstatements.com if you need inspiration

6.4 Which areas and how much detail?

The mission statement and long-term vision, the basic principles and ground rules are generic and by definition high level. But for which areas and to what level of detail should HQ formulate policies and procedures?

Let's say that they should cover all those functional areas in which the company operates and that the amount of detail included should be as small as you can get away with. Areas that spring to mind and that apply to most companies are human resource management, legal affairs, financial affairs[3] IT and procurement. Risk management will probably be in there, too.

The obvious examples in relation to finance are accounting and reporting guidelines. In relation to procurement, you could think of guidelines about how major purchases should be handled and who is responsible for them. In relation to human resources, the policies and procedures would include guidelines on hiring and firing. IT policies and procedures would cover standard systems and safety procedures, for example.

Headquarters' policies and procedures should not be too detailed, but at the same time detailed enough to allow HQ to retain control. Striking the appropriate level of detail needs judgement, but remember: the greater the detail, the more maintenance is required, the more exceptions there are to the rules and the more questions and challenges will be posed. Basically, policies and procedures should be generic and applicable to every unit. For example, be careful not to have headquarters dictate all human resource policies and procedures in a multinational organisation. There can be huge differences between countries and

---

[3] This commonly includes budgeting, reporting, accounts, treasury, cash management and tax planning.

you will do more harm than good by not acknowledging this. Focus on *corporate HR issues* only, such as management development, the basic principles of staff appraisal, expat policies, an employee share ownership plan and high-level employee benefits. Leave the rest to the local business unit managers and their own HR managers. They will come to you anyhow if they need to take decisions that are beyond their own authority.

In certain other areas (such as accounting principles), a high level of detail may be difficult to avoid. Where accounting principles are concerned, there's no need to re-invent the wheel, though. They're all readily available; all HQ needs to do is to choose the principles to which the organisation needs to adhere and elaborate on some.

Business units can develop and maintain their own more detailed policies and procedures in specific areas. There is nothing wrong with this. On the contrary, in some areas you'll have to encourage, or even instruct, them to do so. The only requirement is that these local policies and procedures should not be in conflict with corporate ones.

6.5   Budgets and annual plans

I think it's fair to say that the budget or annual plan lies at the heart of the framework in which the business units operate. The budget or annual plan is a key document in terms of controlling your company. The annual plan describes and quantifies the recurring business, projects and initiatives and the planned capital expenditures.

As for the latter, if the amounts involved are significant and certainly if the expenditure was not planned and therefore not included in the annual plan, the business unit will have to prepare a comprehensive business case to facilitate decision-making.

Headquarters plays a coordinating role in getting the business units to prepare their annual plans at the right time and in an appropriate format and in getting the plans approved at all levels, i.e. by the managing board, the supervisory board and the shareholders, as the case may be.

6.6   Agreement and buy-in

It is very important that HQ and the business units reach agreement on the annual plans and budgets. Any company in which budgets are prepared by headquarters and subsequently imposed on the business units is definitely on the wrong track. Believe me, this happens far too often. A budget is a contract between headquarters and a business unit and therefore needs explicit agreement. It takes two to tango.

As for corporate policies and procedures, although it's true that you don't necessarily need agreement, it does help if the business units *buy into* them. Without a buy-in, it can be difficult to get everyone to comply. In order to get the business units to buy-in, you need at least to properly communicate and explain your policies. Seeking input from business units in developing your policies – especially the more contentious ones – can really help. Remember, though, a company is not a democracy.

6.7   External funding

One of the conditions for any business is the continued support of its financiers[4]. To this end, the latter will require reports

---

[4] These consist of both shareholders (as suppliers of equity capital) and banks (as suppliers of loan capital).

on plans, budgets, progress and on-going activities. The principle applies equally whether the company is privately or publicly owned. It is just the level of detail and the degree of involvement that may differ.

The owners and banks require information not only about how things are going and how the management is responding to changing market conditions. They also want to know about the company's long-term strategy and financial outlook. Obviously, these are all important tasks for headquarters and the managing board.

6.8   Summary and conclusion

So that's it. Headquarters defines and maintains the framework within which the business units operate, HQ ensures that they remain within that framework and HQ reports to the company's owners on how things are going. Couldn't be simpler.

Unfortunately, life is not always that straightforward. You will often need to organise other activities at headquarters, too. But remember, you should only do this if there is a compelling reason to do so. For example, an airline has almost all of its capital locked up in aircraft. An aircraft needs to be in the air as much as possible and can be moved from one business unit to another relatively easily. An aircraft parked on the ground is *eating money*. So it makes a lot of sense for an airline to have a central department that can buy and sell aircraft, move them around according to business needs, register and deregister them, plan and organise major maintenance, and arrange aircraft insurance. Insurance is a significant cost in the aviation industry, where economies of scale can be significant [5]. It is easy to understand that, if every business unit were to perform all these tasks on its own, huge

---

[5] Generally, the larger the fleet, the lower the insurance premium.

economic benefits would be lost.

Other tasks that most large organisations like their headquarters to perform are cash management, currency hedging, arranging large-scale insurance policies and pursuing big lawsuits. These examples speak for themselves. You don't want local operations to hobby around with these things. So as you can see, there's still plenty for HQ to do.

7 Review and control

7.1 Like fire-fighters

For lack of a better name, review and control is the backbone of any company. I have seen many company directors and managers who spend more time fire-fighting than anything else. They run around answering queries from investors, while jumping from one burning platform to the other and launching (but rarely completing) one improvement project after another. These managers will never succeed; they just wear themselves and their subordinates out. By the way, that's how you can easily recognise them: just look at the rate of staff turnover in their immediate surroundings.

A management team on its way to the next burning platform.

Managers who have organised a proper review and control cycle have much easier lives, go home at a decent time of day and live longer. So how does the review and control cycle work?

7.2   Budget = contract

As I discussed in Chapter 6, one of the tasks of headquarters i.e. the managing board, is to agree on an annual plan with the business units. The budgeting process is a crucial step in getting the business under control and sets the stage for the forthcoming year.

Longer term planning (i.e. with a horizon of 3-5 years) can be equally important, especially in businesses with longer revenue cycles, but let's ignore this for the time being. The principle remains the same.

Because of its paramount importance, preparing and agreeing the annual plan requires proper planning and communication, and hence considerable interaction between the managing board at headquarters and the management of the business units in question. The annual plan may well have to go through several rounds of long meetings before agreement is reached on a final version.

Once agreed, the budget has the character of a contract; it tells the business unit what it's allowed to spend and it tells the directors what the unit will deliver and how. It is the road map for all the forthcoming year's activities.

Make sure you standardise the budget format since you have to be able to add up the individual budgets to prepare a consolidated annual plan for your shareholders. In designing the format, of course, you'll align it with your financial and management reporting and you'll include the balanced business score card (see Chapter 12).

As a contract, the budget empowers the business unit to do whatever is needed, within the limits of the company's framework and guidelines, to deliver the agreed performance.

Now that you have a contract, you need to monitor progress to make sure the business unit 'sticks to the agreement'. If they find this difficult, you will need to help and coach the business unit management. In most businesses, the board members cannot afford to sit and wait for a year, in the hope that the 'delivery' will arrive as planned. That's too much to hope for.

7.3   Monitoring

Monitoring should not just be an extensive reporting process involving the desktop analysis of information received from the business units. It's not a one-way street where the unit answers (or tries to dodge) questions from headquarters that keeps asking more and more questions in an attempt to corner the unit. If that is what's happening, you're on the wrong track.

Monitoring should take the form of a constructive dialogue between the managing board and the business unit management. This dialogue should preferably be 'live' and should ideally take place on the business unit's premises, at least some of the time.

In my experience, such meetings are always very enlightening for board members. They are often enjoyed and appreciated by the business units and work as a catalyst for improving business performance. If properly set up, maybe around a site visit, a customer visit or even some socialising, these meetings go a long way in establishing a good company where people enjoy working with each other and are prepared to go the extra mile.

Monitoring needs to have a proper rhythm: monthly, quarterly, semi-annually or annually. Anything is possible. It all depends on the dynamics of the business and the maturity of local management. Although videoconferencing or teleconferencing techniques can be used, nothing beats a "live" local meeting.

A rhythm can also differentiate between 'off' months (like January and February) and 'on' months like March, June and September, so that the reporting and reviewing regime is lighter during 'off' months. Don't be too rigid. As long as there's a rationale behind it, anything goes. It all depends on the circumstances. After all, the less time a business unit spends on internal reporting, the more time it can spend on its customers.

The art is to strike the right balance between allowing business unit managers to actually run and grow their business on the one hand, and the need for HQ to look over their shoulders to monitor, help and coach on the other. This is where the professional judgment and experience of board members comes into play. There's no firm rule, but it's important that you think about it carefully, debate matters with your fellow board members, take a conscious decision, plan it and communicate it.

7.4   Review meetings

An important part of the review dialogue will centre on the progress that is being made, as compared with budget estimates and trends in other areas of the annual plan. Where progress is disappointing, or unexpected events have intervened, business unit managers will have to explain the action they're taking and the members of the managing board will be able to provide directions and give advice. These meetings also allow board members to talk about strategy, issues *they* have on their plate and other corporate developments.

An additional benefit is that the business unit managers get some exposure and hence an opportunity to demonstrate their capabilities and talents to the people who, at the end of the day, dictate their career paths.

To be frank, I don't see how any company can operate without this process, without this constructive structural dialogue between the top and the units. And yet there are lots of businesses that don't have such a structured and planned process .

Don't forget that, at the end of the meetings, you should agree on what should be done by whom (i.e. action points and action-holders) and that the agenda for the next meeting should include reports on the progress made in relation to each of these points.

7.5   Span of control

Depending of the size of the company, the review and control cycle may have to be organised at different levels. The same rule of thumb applies to the span of control for units (departments) as it does to individuals: 5 to 7 entities reporting to the next level is about right. A big, complicated department like Asset Management or a big R&D Division counts as well. An organisation with just two divisions consisting of 5-7 business units each can prove a perfect structure too. Don't be too rigid in designing your organisational structure either, and certainly don't overstretch your span of control. It's better to be safe than sorry.

To do it right, you need to take time and you need to be able to handle unexpected events and growth. You will also have to organise a proper team at Corporate and Divisional HQ level to support your review and control process. This is typically a job for the financial control department.

In a two-tier or three-tier structure, a summary of the actions and issues discussed at a lower level should be on the agenda of meetings held at a higher level, too. It's like a babushka doll: you replicate the process and structure several times. You make the review and control process a corporate policy, to be applied at every level. This is a very effective way for the members of the managing board to ensure that lower management is in control of the units reporting to *them*.

(...) you replicate the process and structure several times (...)

7.6   In summary

The main message here is: structure and plan your meetings with business unit managers, visit them locally and pursue a constructive coaching dialogue with them. Don't overstretch your span of control and don't limit yourself to endless streams of reports and questions 'to save time'.

If you plan this aspect properly, you will find that the review and control process forms the organisational backbone of your company.

7.7   What about HQ support and other departments?

You should plan exactly the same processes for HQ support

departments and an R&D department, for example. They too, need to make annual plans, work to targets, report on their success or otherwise in meeting these targets, and discuss progress with board members. Obviously, the nature of the plans will be different, though. The periodicity will also have to be tailored to the circumstances. This is basically a matter of judgement. In mature and stable situations, once or twice a year may suffice. Where a company is heavily dependent on R&D, for example, the frequency of such meetings will obviously have to be much higher.

Apart from the fact that you need to give support departments a departmental cost budget, most of their performance targets are likely to be qualitative. They will probably relate to developing and improving systems and procedures and making sure they are properly implemented. After all, their prime task is to maintain – and improve – the framework in which the business units operate.

It's also important that you demonstrate to the rest of the company – the people who bring in the money – that HQ support departments are not 'above the law'. They, too, need to be accountable for what they do and have goals to meet, like everyone else.

8   The approach to a corporate reorganisation

8.1   Why restructure? [6]

Organisations constantly evolve. Markets change, new activities are started, and businesses are acquired, sold, closed down or merged. Customers want to know who they are dealing with and investors want to see synergies being realiesed – they want to 'see the money'. This is why the development of a business organisation is something that needs to be handled proactively. You cannot just let a business evolve by itself. You need to reorganise and restructure on a regular basis.

Reorganisations are invariably complex and sometimes downright painful. I have known companies that started to reorganise after a series of acquisitions and that have come to the conclusion six years later that they are still a long way from reaching the finishing line. A poorly implemented reorganisation can be detrimental to a company's profitability as it distracts everyone from their main job: delivering a high-quality service to customers. Also, the biggest enemy of reorganisation is time. Restructuring takes a lot of time and shortcuts often prove dead ends.

When a company performs a wide range of activities, some of these activities will inevitably overlap. There may be overlaps in products or markets, and the various business units may also be fishing in the same pond for resources. Before you know it, you'll find that the units differ in terms of size, degree of maturity and quality of management, without there being any apparent mode of coordination between them, or any form of alignment or logical structure. In other words, if you don't do anything, you'll soon find that your organisation has become a hopelessly entangled mess.

---

[6] The term 'restructuring' is more structure-focused, whereas the term 'reorganisation' is generally used more in connection with people and activities. For the purpose of this book, I don't make a distinction between the two.

You've got yourself a pile of spaghetti instead of a well-oiled machine. The key message here is of course: don't let things get out of hand. The warning signals will get through to you soon enough. Falling profits, high staff attrition, more and more issues escalating to managing board level, a constant flow of unpleasant surprises, unhappy customers: you name it, each one is a recognisable symptom. Be aware that, if you really mess up, it can take years - and a lot of money - to fix it.

Fast-growing organisations in particular, whether they are growing organically or by means of acquisitions, often find themselves in the bottom left-hand quadrant of the next picture at some point. In other words, they end up as a more or less disorganised 'mess', in which business units don't know what other units are doing, where they are competing for the same customers and resources, and whose directors are interested more in expansion than in getting their house in order. This is definitely a place you don't want to be. It's inefficient, opaque for stakeholders and stressful for management. I'll now explain how you can move away from this worst-case situation (bottom left) to a much better place in three steps.

In three steps ...

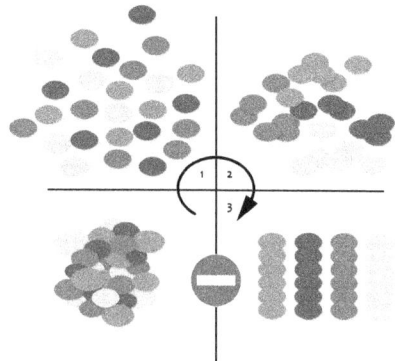

8.2   The first step: define the units

The first step is to define more or less independent business units containing a meaningful part of your activities. Meaningful means manageable in terms of size, location, customer base, type of activity, market and potential to act independently. The latter is an important aspect. If similar companies are operating in the marketplace, that's pretty conclusive proof that the unit can in theory act independently.

This process is complicated and needs brainstorming, workshops and the involvement of all the talent and brainpower that you can get. Bear the long-term vision, mission statement and strategy of the company clearly in mind in doing this. Some activities may no longer tie in with the strategy and may have to be closed down or sold off.

Once you've defined or redefined your business units, you'll have to institutionalise the new structure by formally setting them up. This means giving them a logical (brand) name, picking people to run them and communicating your decisions. Make sure you pick the right people for the managerial positions. Let candidates apply for the jobs and make proper assessments. You should take great care with this. Whilst poor choices made at this stage can be corrected later on, they will cause delays.

If the number of business units becomes too large for your span of control, you will have to group a number of units together into one division. Be very careful to not overstretch your span of control! This clustering should be based on the expected future synergies, in the broadest sense of the word: lower travel expenses for division managers are also a form of synergy.

Don't worry, you won't cut the units loose entirely. The corporate policies and procedures you have put in place, together with the review and control process (see Chapter 7), will help you keep a handle on them. You are taking another big step in creating a good company, though.

The full implementation of this step may take well over a year. It takes time to 'break everyone in'. The amount of time you should reckon with is a full budget and review cycle, i.e. one annual plan and a year's worth of review meetings. By the end of this period, you should have a pretty good view of the quality of the business unit management. Some replacements may already be required.

After this stage, you will find yourself in the top left-hand quadrant of the picture. You will now have a *manageable* company. It's still less than ideal as regards (financial) results, but manageable nonetheless.

8.3   Step 2: turn the screws

With step 1 completed and a proper annual budget and review and control process in place, you can start challenging the financial performance of the 'independent' units. You raise the bar in the second annual plan. By doing so, you force the unit's management to identify synergies with other units and push them actually to *realise* these synergies. You will get the units to work together, not as a goal in itself, but as a means of improving their own performance.

Synergies are what big organisations are all about. Synergy derives from a wide range of sources, from shared systems and increased buying power to shared know-how and common marketing strategies. Synergy is what justifies being part of a group (of companies) to begin with. Without synergy, you might as well split up the group[7] and leave investors to choose whether to place the individual businesses in one and the same investment portfolio.

It's very hard to impose synergies top down and any attempt to do so is bound to run into a lot of opposition. People always find reasons to resist change. That's why you need to create a vested interest, a drive, in order to realise synergies. So if you push the business units' managements hard enough to improve their financial performance, 'turn the screw' as it were, they'll soon find out that working together with other units may not be such a bad idea after all. In fact, they may discover that it is the easiest way of improving their own unit's performance and earning a bonus.

Of course, there is nothing wrong with the managing board coordinating this process proactively, by helping the business units and setting priorities. On the contrary. You will see that there are two sorts of gains to be made: quick, big ones, the 'low hanging fruit', and the 'long shots'. Let the business units focus first and foremost on the former. Forget the latter, for now.

Ensure that worthwhile initiatives end up in the business units' annual plans and make sure you monitor follow-up and progress. The more actions are initiated by the units themselves, the greater the chance of success. All you need do is make sure the business unit's managers have an incentive to make it all work by linking their bonus to the 'delivery' of the annual plan (see chapter 19).

---

[7] GE is probably the exception to the rule, the quality and culture of the management being the 'synergy' between the various group companies.

8.4   Step 3: the finishing touch

The third and final step in the process is basically a refinement of the second step. It brings the company into the situation as illustrated in the bottom right-hand section of the picture. The result is a perfectly structured organisation, in which all business units that have the most synergies are fully aligned and work together, and all significant synergies are realised. Typically, the completion of this final step takes another budget and review cycle.

All in all, it takes three cycles plus preparation and planning to go from a disorganised disjointed 'mess' to a transparent, well-managed and *efficient* group of companies. Let's say 3.5 years at most. It can definitely be done quicker, depending on your starting point and other circumstances, but believe me, it *does* take time. The key message remains of course: don't take the spaghetti route: don't let things get out of hand so much that you have to start in the bottom-left quadrant.

8.5   The classic mistake

Now, let me warn you for the classic mistake. Organisations go through step one, define what they reckon is the ideal break-up into business units, form a perfect combination of units into divisions, and realise - on paper - all the synergies they can think of. They may even dream up a single, group-wide ERP [8] system. Some companies think they can solve all their organisational problems by designing and implementing this type of system. And because these companies are in a hurry to get everything done, they can't wait. They go from the bottom left to the bot-

---

[8] Enterprise resource planning; a fully integrated and interfaced software system for the entire company.

54

DO NOT ENTER That sign is there for a reason...

tom right of the picture in one big step. Why not?

I'll tell you why not: because there's a 'no entry' sign between the two compartments. That sign is there for a reason. Believe me: trying to go from a pile of spaghetti to a perfectly aligned dish in one step simply does not work. The evidence is there: lots of people have tried and they've all failed! You cannot impose all these changes in one step without going through a step-by-step learning process with your staff. Remember: they're used to working in a pile of spaghetti!

I have seen my share of reorganisations. The vast majority of them have been failures. Every single time, the reason has been that the directors could not resist the temptation of moving from the bottom left to the bottom right in a single step.

So remember the picture. I saw it somewhere and never forgot it. For many years now, I have jotted it on whiteboards over and over again in order to explain how companies should re-structure themselves without making the classic mistake.

9   The stakeholder model

As we all know, companies have many different stakeholders. I am not going to deal extensively with stakeholder models
in this chapter, nor will I be attempting to convince you that all
stakeholders are equally important. As you can read in paragraph
9.3 my message is a little bit different, but let's go briefly through
the basics first.

9.1   This about sums it up

The illustration below shows a typical set of corporate stakeholders.

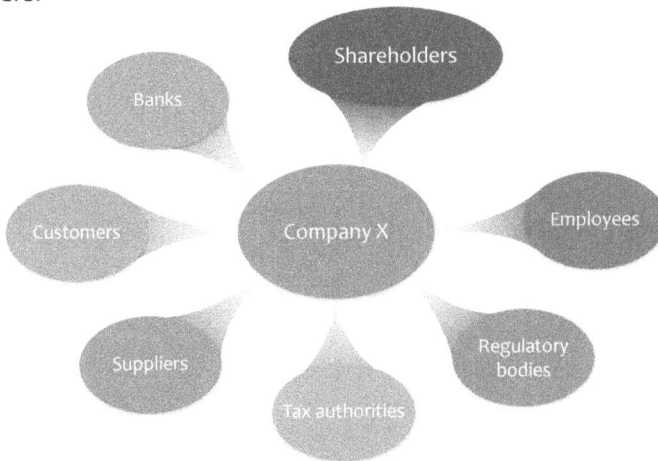

- The shareholders want high returns with low risk. The returns may just be dividends, but many shareholders base the
  estimates of their returns on an exit scenario (i.e. the pros-
  pect of selling their shares at a higher price than they bought
  them for). In the latter case, especially if the time horizon is
  short, this will very much govern their behaviour.

- The employees want job security, fair pay, pleasant work and nice colleagues. They want to learn and develop their talents. I deliberately say 'fair' pay. Do bear in mind that giving a disgruntled employee a pay rise only works for a very short period. Other staff *wanahaves* tend to be more important and certainly more sustainable.
- Regulatory bodies want you to comply with their rules, to be transparent and open about how you run your operations. And they want you to pay your membership fee.
- The tax authorities want you both to comply with the relevant tax laws and to pay your taxes.
- Suppliers want your patronage. They want to charge you as much as they can get away with, and they want you to pay for your deliveries. Most of them want you to come back next time.
- Customers want your goods or services at the best possible price, on time and with the right quality.
- The banks want to be paid interest on their loans and preferably don't want to run any risk at all. Even more, banks want to sell you all kinds of complex financial products that generate immediate fees and bonuses. But let's not go there. Not here.

It's not much more complicated than that.

9.2   Creating shareholder value

Early stakeholder theories consistently centred on shareholders and the creation of *shareholder value*. Later theories emphasised the importance of *all* stakeholders and how company directors need to balance the interests of all stakeholders in order to keep everybody happy.

These two approaches are not mutually exclusive. In fact,

they're fully complementary. As a company director, you need, first and foremost, to keep your shareholders happy. You can only do that by keeping *all the stakeholders happy.* If you upset some or all of your other stakeholders, believe me, you'll eventually upset the shareholders. If your best managers or salesmen walk away, your profitability will take a dive. If your banks don't want to lend you money, you'll have to go begging to your shareholders. If you dodge the tax rules, you'll get fined. One way or another, the shareholders will eventually find out about if one of your stakeholders is disgruntled. They won't be happy about it because they will feel the pain in their long-term returns.

9.3   The time factor

Now, the dimension that can disturb this logical balance is *time.* If shareholders have a short-term horizon and want to sell their investment soon, they may not be unduly worried about any staff, suppliers or customers who are getting unhappy over time.

If the shareholders are planning on exiting before the business is really harmed by the effects of unhappy stakeholders, you may find yourself in a difficult spot trying to balance all the interests. That's why, in many cases, shareholders give directors a piece of the pie in the form of shares or stock options. The idea is to give board members a stronger financial interest in the shareholders' agenda and especially in their time horizon. In other words, the object is to make sure that you're on their side.

In a short-term exit scenario that is not uncommon with investment funds, venture capitalists or hedge funds, shareholders will have little patience, will not be interested in long-term investments and long-winded reorganisations and will be pushing for short-term improvements in the company's financials (i.e.

cash flows). You will therefore find it much more difficult to balance their interests with those of the other stakeholders, especially the employees. And you will hardly have enough time to do things properly.

This is an area in which I cannot really do much to help you. However, if you're conscious of the time factor and you manage to maintain your integrity, you've won half the battle. You'll be in for some tough discussions with the shareholders. The main need, I would say, is to have a proper discussion with your shareholders before you even embark on a process like this. Try to get time to do things properly, because if time horizons are incompatible, you may be embarking on a mission impossible.

10 The legal structure versus the management structure

10.1 A Christmas tree

In terms of their legal structure, many large multinationals look like huge Christmas trees. Often, they're not even very symmetric ones: wonky trees with missing branches, ugly gaps and lots of dead wood. Many of these structures are the unavoidable results of their past history, such as:

* setting up separate entities for new activities; legally segregating new, yet unknown, liabilities and risks from their existing core business;
* tax planning; setting up (asset) companies in tax havens, moving activities to jurisdictions with low tax rates, moving holding companies to countries with participation exemptions and low withholding taxes on dividends;
* legal requirements on shareholdings; e.g. minimum shareholding by nationals, minimum ownership (and control) by Europeans [9], etc;
* mergers and acquisitions.

The latter often increases the complexity of the group's legal structure as each new acquisition adds another Christmas tree to it.

(...) with missing branches, ugly gaps and lots of dead wood (...)

---

[9] For example, EU-based airlines must be at least 50% owned and controlled by European citizens.

61

10.2 And then business takes over

So your company's legal structure gradually evolves. And then the business starts to organise, reorganise, combine, split and reshuffle activities in such a way that the group performs best *in operational terms*. This means performing in such a way that most of the potential synergies are realised (see Chapter 8).

After one or more acquisitions, the management structure, as the optimum operational structure, may in fact look completely different from the legal structure. This adds to the complexity of running the business: it adds to the cost and raises the risks of errors being made. There's often much more to it than meets the eye.

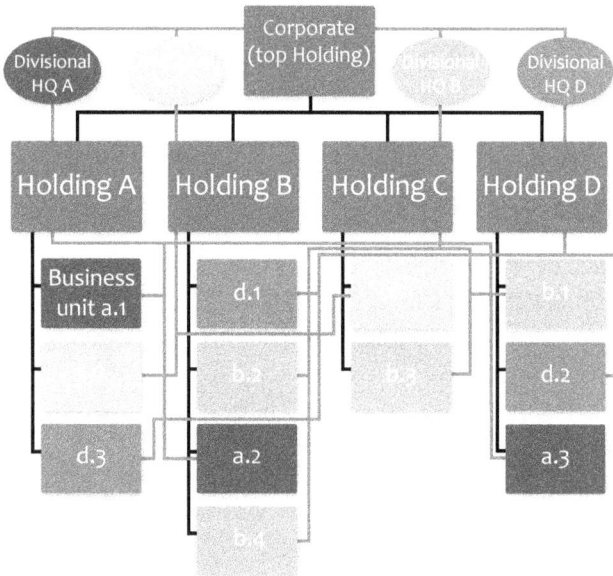

Legal structure inconsistent with management structure: complex

10.3   Aligning structures

The lesson here is that every company needs to make a con-scious effort to align the legal structure as closely as possible with the management structure. Although this may not be en-tirely feasible, the closer they are the better. Bear in mind that a sound business has a simple and transparent structure.

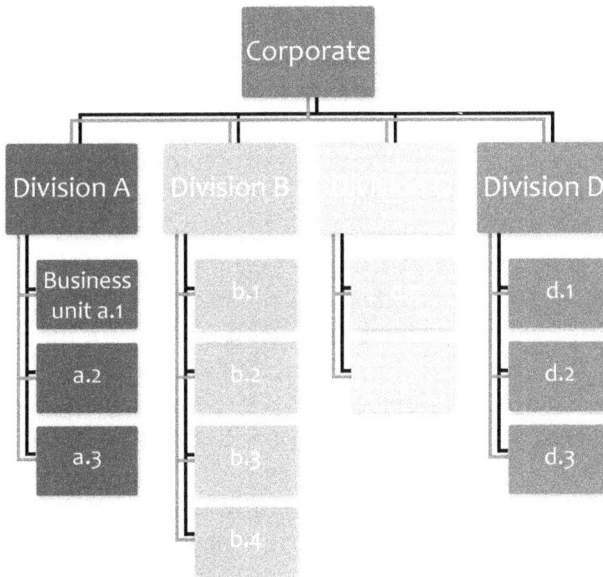

Legal structure equals management structure: simple.

This also implies that you need to constantly adapt and streamline your legal structure, adapt it to reorganisations and management changes, and cut out dead wood, i.e. liquidate dor-mant companies.

Of course, you need to take tax advice in all this, but do make sure that your tax advisors don't take control of this process as they tend not to take proper account of the day-to-day organisational complexities that they create:

- Inconsistency between the legal and management structures introduces ambiguity in responsibilities and liabilities. Ambiguity is a breeding ground for mistakes. Ideally, each business unit should be placed in a separate limited liability company and the business unit manager should be the formal - statutory - director of that company. This makes it all very straightforward and ensures that legal responsibility (vis-à-vis the outside world) rests with the same person as the related management responsibility *within* the company. Make the 'formal structure' as consistent as possible with the review and control process structure (see Chapter 7).
- Adding legal responsibility to a person's day-to-day management responsibilities increases his or her sense of responsibility in general and encourages ethical conduct.
- Financial audits, including the signing off of representation letters, generally follows the *legal* structure, not the management structure.
- Inconsistency between the legal structure and management structure creates additional paperwork – 'getting hold of the right signature' - in dealings with the outside world, i.e. banks, customers, suppliers, authorities, etc. Additional paperwork creates additional cost, delays and distraction, and raises the risk of error.

This all really means nothing more than adhering to the principle of keeping things nice and simple. The simpler the structure, the less ambiguity there is and the less risk there is of errors occurring, and hence the more effective it is.

I have been in contact with a multinational company in which a local chief accountant was *legally* responsible for as much as 75% of the group's operations. This is absolutely ridiculous. I have also seen a company in which a junior manager had overstepped the line in his behaviour towards a major customer. When the company defended itself by saying that 'he was only a junior manager', the customer's lawyer pointed out that the man happened to have been formally appointed as the director of one of the divisional holding companies. It was extremely painful.

10.4   Complex tax structures

Many big multinational companies have very complex legal structures for tax reasons. The aim is to reduce the corporate tax burden and thus to increase net income. This is a very legitimate aspiration. Moreover, a CFO would not be doing a good job if he/she did not make tax efficiency one of the priorities.

Let me put things into perspective, though. In order to pay tax, you've first got to make a profit. At least that's the situation in most countries. So focus first and foremost on making a profit. And only then start worrying about tax efficiency.

Secondly, in every country where you own legal entities, even if they are not active, you have to prepare and file local accounts and comply with all the local tax legislation. This all means recurring annual accounting, legal and tax fees. You may even need some local 'substance'; letterbox companies are not always permissible. This often also means holding local shareholder and Board meetings, both of which take up time and energy. All these activities have no added value for your business and are in fact unwelcome distractions. Don't underestimate the direct - and especially the indirect - cost of all this.

Thirdly, as illustrated in section 10.3, complexity makes responsibilities ambiguous and raises the risk of error. Errors are very costly to correct, as you know.

You therefore need to perform a full cost-benefit analysis of this issue before creating a complex structure and should update this analysis on a regular basis. Although it's impossible to estimate the cost of potential errors and mistakes, a qualitative evaluation is probably the least you should do.

The analysis should bear in mind the fact that a tax dollar is in many respects a 'cheaper' dollar than a dollar spent on consultants and recurring fees, or worse, on the correction of an error. This is because many companies are valued on the basis of a *multiple* of EBIT[10] or EBITDA[11]. Bank covenants, too, are generally based on EBITDA (e.g. the debt-service coverage ratio). In other words, a dollar spent on a consultant reduces the EBITDA and thus ends up being multiplied, possibly by as much as 7 or 8.

A tax dollar is just a dollar, though. Food for thought?

---

[10] Earnings before interest and tax
[11] Earnings before interest, tax, depreciation and amortisation

11.   Matrix organisations

11.1   Great on paper

A matrix organisation - an organisation with multiple, equally important, 'lines of control' - looks great on paper. That's probably why management consultants love it. It creates flexibility, enables a coordinated approach and eliminates sub-optimal, silo thinking. In practice, however, it is extremely complex. This may be another reason why consultants like it so much: complexity means advice. Bucket loads of it. However, you immediately recognise the word 'complex' as being the direct opposite of simple. Need I say more? Don't do a matrix organisation!

I'm not saying it's impossible for a matrix organisation to work. I'm sure there are good examples of where it works well. I am just saying that I wouldn't do it. It's too complex; there's too much hassle, too many people involved in everything, too many meetings with each other instead of with customers, too much internal focus, and not enough engagement with the outside world. So it's not for me, thank you very much.

11.2   How 'complex' can run you to the ground

Philips Electronics used to have a matrix organisation. The basis was a national (country) organisation overlaid by a product division structure. To make things worse, they also had a strong functional organisation, with finance, research and production. In fact it was almost a three-dimensional matrix.

Both the national management and the division management consisted of a technical director and a commercial director, both of whom had direct lines to the Board of Directors. Needless to say it was all very complex. So much so that it made the company completely ineffective and seriously contributed to its near collapse in the early 1990's.

A couple of years later, the then CEO, Cor Boonstra[12], claimed that 'Philips is like a plate of spaghetti. Personally, I prefer a plate of neatly arranged asparagus.' [13] A man after my heart!

The problems at Philips started with the basic matrix. The rest just exacerbated the complexity and the mess. Having two lines of authority is like having two captains on the same ship. It doesn't work. It's like a child playing off one parent against the other. If they don't get what they want from Mum, they go to Dad. Naturally, Mum's most annoyed if Dad then gives in.

11.3   Synergies

As a managing board, you have to choose how you are going to manage your organisation. An operational matrix avoids a choice and is often a bad compromise. So how do you set out your lines of authority? Are they based on geography, products, markets or something else? How do you decide what's best?

The answer is *synergy*. It is where you expect to obtain the most synergy that decides which line you take and what operations you place under the same leadership. If there are no clear and significant operational synergies, you might as well let location and size determine your choice. There's nothing wrong with that.

Make sure you look at synergy in its broadest sense. It's about much more than just creating economies of scale or saving costs

---

[12] Director and Chairman of the Board at Philips, 1994-2001
[13] *Let's make things better*, Marcel Metze, January 1998.

in other ways. Synergy can also be derived from having the same customers, the same *type* of customers, the same type of employees, the same business model, brand, logistics, etc.

The crux of synergy is that combining activities and placing them under the same leadership makes you more efficient and/or more effective. Ultimately, therefore, it saves costs or yields more revenue – and preferably both.

11.4   The long screwdriver

Many 'matrix' organisations these days are a combination of *geography* (or product/market) on the one hand and *function* on the other. I know large corporations where the finance department handles all financial matters, the HR department is responsible for all personnel-related issues, Legal Affairs deals with all transactions requiring a written contract and so forth. These companies end up being micromanaged by HQ support departments with a very long screwdriver. It's frightening.

11.5   Firm lines and dotted lines

'In my book', the best structure is a simple line organisation with functional dotted lines. This means that both the financial manager in a business unit as well as the HR manager, for example, reports to the business unit manager.

This implies that, if the business unit's financial reports arrive too late, or if they're inaccurate, it's the business unit manager's responsibility, not the CFO's. This is the only way of making the job of a CFO bearable, by the way. Why should you let the local business unit manager off the hook? It's his (or her) business, and they're his or her numbers, so he or she should be on top of them. The business unit manager has a crucial role to play in making sure that the unit performs well, and that this performance is reflected in the books. He or she is best placed to perform this role. So make the business unit manager responsible, the 'owner' of the problem. This means that if he or she doesn't understand numbers at all, they may not be the right man or woman for the job. A good course in 'finance for non-financial managers' may do the trick, but it's imperative for a manager to have a decent understanding of finance. You cannot run a business without it.

Incidentally, treating the unit managers in this way will also create the right breeding ground for future board members.

A Chief Financial Officer cannot dodge his or her responsibility to the outside world, though. A CFO is perceived as being responsible for all aspects of the company's financial management, but internally, he should delegate a big part of the responsibility to the business unit manager.

Clear, solid lines are paramount, but don't underestimate the importance of dotted lines. There will be a dotted line linking the CFO with the business unit's financial manager. The CFO will play a role in hiring and, if necessary, firing the financial manager. The CFO will be one of the annual appraisers and will, of course, define the framework in which the financial manager works, i.e. the time lines, accounting principles, formats, policies and main procedures. In some industries (depending on the nature of the business) and in some circumstances, that dotted line can become pretty substantial. However, regard the solid line as your principal line of authority, and stick to the principle of the business unit manager being responsible for his entire business, within the company's framework, of course. Don't turn your organisation into a matrix. As I said, it introduces ambiguity.

A good dotted-line rapport is essential for an organisation to work effectively. The CFO wants to know how good the business unit's financial manager is, and wants to be sure the latter keeps a straight back when the business unit manager puts pressure on him or her 'to make the budget numbers' and earn an annual bonus. This is a delicate situation that the business unit's financial manager needs to be able to handle and the CFO should help out here. Exactly the same principle applies to human resources, legal affairs and other support services.

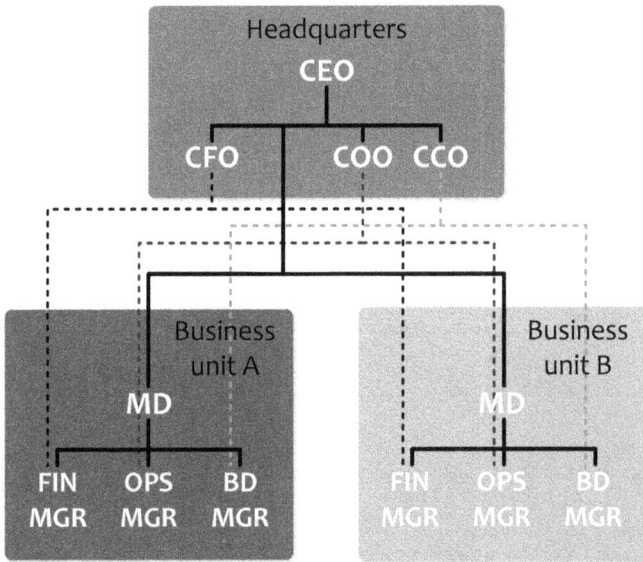

A styled example of a line organisation with dotted line relations.

12 Financial accounting, management accounting and tax accounting

12.1 Financial accounting

Financial accounting means accounting and reporting based on an official set of accounting rules or accounting principles. The way in which companies record their transactions and prepare their financial statements is based on a commonly accepted set of accounting principles. This ensures that users of financial statements know what they're looking at and can make comparisons between companies.

It sounds simple, but it's not. The 'rule books' of accounting principles have become incredibly complicated. Not only are they as thick as telephone directories, but you need to be a specialist in order to interpret them. In some cases, the rules are ambiguous and allow choices. Even certified accountants need specialists within their own breed to clarify the rules.

Much to my dismay, accountants are often even involved in *structuring* transactions and drafting contracts, to ensure the best possible results from an accounting viewpoint. It's a slippery slope: accounting should follow the business, not the other way around.

There are also differences between the various *sets* of principles. The most commonly used accounting principles are US GAAP and IFRS. The USA still clings on to its own rules, whilst IFRS is now generally used in the rest of the world. Some progress is being made in converging the two sets of principles, so as to create a single world standard for the preparation of financial statements.

12.2   Management accounting

Management accounting is the term commonly used for all sorts of financial statements used *within* a company. These are the numbers for which there are no rules. Anything goes. Any company, and any manager within that company, can define their management accounts according to their own wishes. They can invent their own rules, periodicity and formats.

The management accounts are used for internal management purposes and don't go beyond the company itself. This means that there is no huge 'rule book', that no real expertise is required, there is no redundant information, no hassle and, best of all, no external adviser is needed to interpret the rules and no external auditor needs to opine on the numbers. Isn't that great? Actually, no. It's not.

12.3   The management accounts pitfall

The problem with management accounts is that, if you let them run away with themselves, you can easily create an inside and an outside world for numbers. Before you know it, your managers are taking decisions based on numbers that are not consistent with – or worse, bear no relation whatsoever with – the numbers that you, the members of Board, publish and are held accountable for by your external stakeholders.

One of the consequences is that, when you hold your regular review meetings[14] with the relevant business unit manager, you will spend most of the time trying to reconcile the numbers that the unit is proudly presenting with those you yourself are familiar

---

[14] See Chapter 7: Review and Control.

with. Clearly, this will not be conducive to the effectiveness of the meeting.

One of the classic problems here is that business unit managers (and sales managers in general) very conveniently tend to have no idea of revenue recognition policies. They simply count everything they can as revenue. Before long, the business unit manager thinks he's well above budget because he's also counting future revenue, and perhaps even future contracts. In reality, he may not even be *close* to meeting his budget for the period under discussion. It's a very awkward situation, to say the least.

12.4   Merge financial accounts and management accounts

There are two lessons to be learned here.
1. First of all, let the financial manager, or a financial controller close to him (and not some kind of commercial controller reporting to the commercial manager) prepare the management accounts.
2. Secondly, make sure the management accounts always reconcile with the financial accounts i.e. the financial statements.

The simplest (hence my favourite) way of achieving the latter is simply by using your financial statements as the *basis* for your management accounts. Use your official profit & loss (P&L) account format as the highest level of aggregation for your management accounts and create more detail – by breaking down P&L lines – where this is useful. This will guarantee direct reconciliation and ensure that everyone is using the same principles. Everyone will end up talking the same 'numbers language', with only one version of the truth. Believe me, that's priceless.

12.5 Economic profit

However detailed your P&L account may be, it is of course a bit of a meagre basis on which to manage your company. There are two additional things you can do to give your managers all the tools they need.

The first is to include a separate cost line item in your P&L account, after net operating profit after tax (NOPAT), that deals with the cost of capital used by a business unit. The cost (%) is the required rate of return for shareholders, and the capital consists of the fixed assets and working capital employed by the business. Once you deduct these costs, the remaining profit becomes the value that the business is creating. This value is often referred to as the *economic profit*.

The method is called the EVA method ('economic value added'). Especially in a capital-intensive business, it is extremely important to manage your capital employed. You need to look at the fixed assets used by the business units and the outstanding working capital (especially accounts receivable, prepayments and inventories). Examining the EVA of your business units is a good way of doing exactly that.

Connoisseurs like to adjust the NOPAT and the capital employed for all kind of items that are capable of distorting your outcome. Some theories suggest up to 40 or 50 potential corrections. Don't go there! Don't make your model too complex. People will get confused and will not understand how the system works. It will not be effective as a result. Again, keep things simple.

One correction that I *would* consider making involves recording the market value of assets instead of their book value. Significant differences between market and book values are not uncommon and can lead to the wrong management decisions if not addressed in the EVA calculation.

12.6   The business dashboard

The second thing I would recommend is that you design and use a 'business dashboard', i.e. a balanced business score card (BBSC)[15] to complement your P&L account. According to the theory, a BBSC is a dashboard that looks at a business from four different angles. Don't be too rigid about it, though. Three or five may work better for your business. The four angles discussed in the theory are:
- Financial
- Customer
- Business processes
- The learning organisation / innovation

You need to define a couple (not too many: five is fine) of key performance indicators (KPIs) for each of these dimensions. Remember, knowledge in the form of hard facts and figures are the basis for good decisions. Make sure your measurements are relevant, reliable, objective and that you have a simple system in place that delivers them to you every month.

It goes without saying that the financial measurements need to reconcile to the financial statements. Make sure you include cash flow as one of your financial KPIs (EBITDA can be a good enough proxy for cash flow). You cannot manage the financial side of your business on the EVA P&L account alone.

Depending on your business, the indicators could include the number of staff employed, the number of FTEs,[16] the number of days of sick leave, the order backlog, the stock turnover, the average number of days during which receivables are outstanding, etc. The possibilities are infinite.

---

[15] *The Balanced Scorecard: Translating Strategy into Action.* Robert S. Kaplan and David P. Norton. Harvard Business School Press, Boston, 1996.
[16] The staff complement expressed in terms of full-time equivalents

Make sure the indicators are relevant to your vision and strategy, as targets will need to be set for them in line with your vision and strategy. The BBSC, the targets and the actions that need to be taken to attain these targets will be included in the annual plan.

You'll need to spend quite a bit of time and energy in designing a good BBSC, and also some considerable effort in implementing it, but it's well worthwhile. Make sure you involve your business unit managers in the design of their own BBSCs. Even better, get them to do it themselves. Don't make the mistake of dictating the detail. And don't make it too detailed to begin with. It must be effective above all else. Also, be aware that a consolidated BBSC can only cover the generic KPIs. Every business unit needs its own specific indicators.

How about this for a business dashboard?

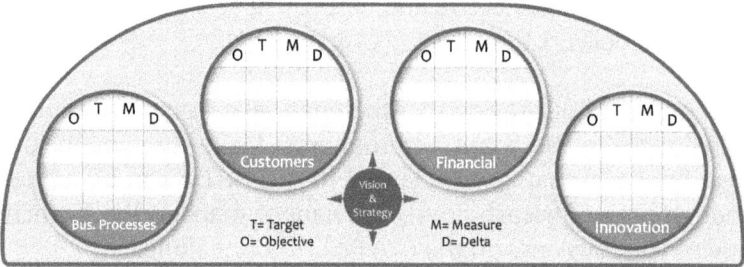

12.7 Everything you need at your fingertips

You'll find that, if you have a good BBSC and EVA P&L account at your fingertips, you should be able to hold your managers to account exactly as you wish. In turn, your managers will have great tools for managing their businesses.

Comparisons between actual outcomes and targets (financial budget or KPIs), will be the main dishes on the menu of your regular review meetings. Plus the action points from the last meeting, of course.

Simple. Everything's coming together nicely now.

12.8 Tax accounting

A third type of accounting is tax accounting. The tax accounts are almost always based on the financial accounts. Basically, they are no more than a series of adjustments to the financial accounts, i.e. the official financial statements. Be warned, however: it's an area prone to complication and mess.

The differences between financial accounting and tax accounting are partly unavoidable. For example, certain costs may not be tax-deductible, which means that the numbers in your financial accounts will need to be adjusted. These adjustments are *permanent*. Similarly, tax rules may impose a different *timing* of certain costs and revenues compared with the financial statements. These differences are *temporary* and will disappear over time.

In practice, most differences between the tax accounts and your financial accounts are temporary and *voluntary*. For example, a company may be allowed to depreciate a building over

10 years for tax purposes, while in its financial statements the same building is depreciated over a more realistic period of 40 years. Governments tend to allow this kind of thing to encourage spending and construction, and hence to stimulate the economy. It helps companies to delay tax payments and therefore improves their short-term cash flow.

The income statement will still show the entire tax *charge*; deferred taxes do need to be recorded as a tax expense and should be stated on the balance sheet as a liability. The discrepancy between the two accounts will disappear after 40 years, hence its classification as a *temporary* difference. A company may elect to not use the tax facility.

All the above is perfectly fine and can be very worth doing given the time value of money. The only advice I have here is to create discrepancies between your tax accounts and your financial accounts only if they are worth it. The benefits are easy to calculate, but the costs of complexity are not. So make sure the benefits are glaring at you in the face. Be wary of needless complexity and hobby horses. Life is complex enough as it is. Before you know it, you will have built a playground for internal and external tax advisors and most of the input for your tax returns will be in a couple of peoples' heads. This is a situation you want to avoid. It distracts you from your really important goal: becoming an outstanding company providing the best quality service to your customers.

13 Shared service centres for accounting

13.1 Is the hype over?

Maybe I've been too busy working on other things in recent times, but I have a feeling that the 'hype' surrounding shared services centres for accounting has died down a bit. If that's true, I'm not surprised. If it's only my perception, then here's my take on how we can kill the hype now and bring things back into proportion.

At the beginning of this century, following the dramatic improvement in data communication and the introduction of web-based applications, shared service centres seemed to be the way forward for efficient accounting. Some companies believed not only that they would save a lot of money thanks to the economies of scale they brought with them, but also that they would improve the quality and timeliness of financial and management information, and enhance financial control. Some even were convinced that shared services centres would help them to be SOX-compliant.[17]

13.2 The accounting factory

In reality, a shared service centre for accounting is nothing more than an accounting factory. *Factory* is the key word.

---

[17] The Sarbanes-Oxley Act of 2002, also known as the 'Public Company Accounting Reform and Investor Protection Act', commonly called Sarbanes–Oxley or SOX, is a US federal law which set new or enhanced standards for all US public company boards, management and public accounting firms. It is named after its sponsors, US Senator Paul Sarbanes and US Representative Michael Oxley. The law was enacted in response to a series of major financial scandals (e.g. Worldcom and Enron).

A service centre processes accounting-related entries, preferably en masse. In other words, it's an old-fashioned mass production plant. Don't even think about it if the volumes are not big.

The thing with these service centres is that they are by definition remote. They process accounting-related entries away from where the transactions occur, away from the action. They are preferably located in regions where accounting staff earn low salaries. This may even be another continent in a different time zone. So problem number one is distance and time. The biggest challenge here is not so much the logistic component: IT and communication technology will help you with this. Rather, it's what I'd call the 'touch and feel' factor.

As you may remember from the section on centralisation and decentralisation, I feel strongly about people having to be close to an issue in order to handle it effectively and efficiently. The same rule applies to accounting. The closer the records are to the transaction, the more accurate and timely they tend to be.

13.3   Different jurisdictions?

The other issue is that, especially in an *international* environment, the centre will be located in a different jurisdiction from which the transactions take place. Another jurisdiction means other employment laws and payroll taxes, different VAT regimes and corporation tax laws, and different statutory requirements. This implies that either the service centre needs to have expertise on local rules or it needs to organise local support from consultants. Although the latter is probably the most practical, it is often the more expensive solution. This will cause part, or maybe even all, of the economies of scale generated by your shared service centre to leak away. That's something to bear in mind before you even start.

13.4   Conclusion

In summary, shared service centres for accounting (or for other services for that matter) only work if two important conditions are met:
- there must be large volumes of identical transactions, *and*
- the operations and its shared service centre must be located within one and the same jurisdiction.

If these two conditions are not met, a shared service centre will not work. Forget it.

All successful shared service centres (and there are many, that's undeniable) are operated by big companies performing a large number of highly similar transactions (for the necessary volumes) and are *national* not cross-border shared service centres. Everything else has been tried, but I have yet to hear the first success story.

14 Internal suppliers and captive markets

14.1   Another classic pitfall

Large organisations often have different businesses in the same value chain. In most of these cases, the managing board decides to make it compulsory for one business unit to purchase from another business unit within the group. That seems logical. What greater synergy could there be than selling goods and services to one another? Why give outsiders business that you as group can do yourself?

There's nothing wrong with buying from a fellow group company. It generates work, keeps people employed, increases your scale and keeps profit margins in-house that otherwise would go to outsiders. However, bear in mind that, as a group, you have not made a penny until you have sold your products or services to the outside world.

This is not the contentious point that I am driving at, though. I'm interested particularly *in human behaviour*. People, whether they're internal suppliers or internal customers, start to act differently when they are *compelled* to buy goods and services from one another. The word *differently* means 'contrary to the group's interests'. This can be very detrimental in the long run. So much so, in fact, that I have made avoiding this particular pitfall one of my basic principles.

14.2   The lazy supplier

The first problem is that, by *forcing* units to do business with each other, you are making life too easy for internal suppliers. They will grow lazy. Service-quality levels will go down and costs will go up.

You will even see that external customers will be given priority over internal ones.

They will grow lazy.

Since internal customers have nowhere else to go and external customers can walk away anytime, internal suppliers always work harder for the latter. This applies particularly if you (the members of the managing board) have given the unit a stiff target to meet for external business, which you probably have.

Don't even be surprised if your internal supplier makes its internal customers pay more than its external customers for exactly the same product, thereby effectively subsidising third party business.

And be ready to face a barrage of complaints from your business unit managers that you will have to resolve.

14.3   A barrage of complaints

This brings me to a second problem. The complaints will undoubtedly be rightful in many cases, but weaker business units may use it as an excuse to hide their own failures. You have handed them a perfect excuse for failure, and perhaps even for not reaching their targets. Looking into the merits of all these complaints is something you just don't want to get drawn into. So avoid the situation in the first place.

14.4   Conclusion

I know it's very tempting to force internal purchases upon your business units. However, it's the beginning of the end, so don't do it.

Make sure your internal suppliers are competitive in both price and service delivery. You may want to give them the right to match external offers and make them the group's *preferred* suppliers. They're family after all! But don't give them guaranteed business.

And don't worry about what such a decision may do to your overall business. You'll see that internal suppliers will get most, if not all, of the internal business anyway, thanks to contacts, the 'family feeling' within the company, and thanks to their status as preferred suppliers.

If they don't get the internal business, believe me, you have another problem on your hands that needs your immediate attention. That problem would have come out sooner or later in any case. At least you now know.

Part III.   Additional take-aways

15   Understanding cultural differences

15.1   Cultures and business

This is one of my hobbyhorses. The link between culture and business is so interesting (and useful) that I think it should be addressed by any general management book.

I am not going to try and tell you all there is to know about cultures and their effect on business. I couldn't do it if I wanted to. I merely want to make you aware and give you some hints. I want to alert you to the fact that cultural differences have a bigger impact on your business than you may think. If you acknowledge the differences, you're already halfway to dealing with them. Ignore them at your peril. If you're about to deal with a completely new culture, prepare yourself. Unless you want to learn the hard way, that is.

Cultural differences exist everywhere. They exist between cities, between regions, between countries and between continents. But they also exist between companies and sometimes even between different units of the same company.

Cultural differences between companies in the same group can be a big hindrance to the attainment of synergy. Take the merger between the ABN and AMRO banks in the Netherlands in 1990. It took them over ten years to 'digest' the merger and become a single company with one culture and one 'face' in the marketplace. The differences in culture were enormous at first; even today, more than 20 years later, the remainders of the two original components are sometimes still visible. Arrogance, for example, is an attribute from one of the two original banks (I forgot which one) that survived the merger very well.

15.2 Culture theory

According to a prominent theory[18], you can measure every culture in terms of five dimensions. By scoring a culture in these dimensions, you can learn to understand it. This makes it easier to predict the impact that a given cultural background has on people and to foresee the reactions and behaviour of individuals from that culture. As we know, understanding reactions and behaviour is the key to being effective, to 'getting things done'. This applies not just internally within the organisation, but also in your approach to the market. An advertising campaign that pushes the wrong 'cultural buttons' can ruin your business for a very long time.

In short, and in my own words, the five dimensions are:

- Power distance: how do people deal with hierarchic authority?
- Masculinity/femininity: how do people deal with success and status?
- Avoidance of uncertainty: what do people do to avoid unclear situations?
- Individualism/collectivism: do people set themselves apart from a group and display their individual personalities or do they prefer to act together?
- Long-term v. short-term orientation: are people focussed on getting food on the table today or are they more concerned about their retirement?

15.3 Some interesting examples

Most behaviour stems from a combination of these five di-

---

[18] See Hofstede's *Cultures and Organizations: Software of the Mind* (New York: McGraw-Hill, 2004).

mensions. Let me give you a couple of examples from my own experience.

Employee of the month

The Americans invented this 'motivation booster' some time ago and tried to export it. It failed hopelessly in the Netherlands. Not only that, but it was actually counterproductive. The poor chaps acclaimed the company's 'employee of the month' were mocked, their pictures on noticeboards decorated with beards and moustaches, and they were seen as 'brown-nosers'.

RESERVED for employee of the month

Nobody in the Netherlands wants to be seen as being better than everyone else. Next month, everyone made quite sure they wouldn't be named. Imagine what that does to your business efficiency.

This Dutch behaviour follows from a combination of low masculinity and high collectivism.

Giving the example

In Nigeria (and most other African cultures), the boss is the boss. Different rules apply to him than to the workers. For example, the boss shouldn't get his hands dirty. So if a Director of Engineering shows his workers how to disassemble an aircraft gearbox, he is on his way to losing their respect. The boss should sit behind a desk or in meetings and should definitely not get his hands and shirt greasy. In most European countries, however, the same act would hugely impress the employees and would help the manager to gain support and respect. Not in Africa.

In short, power distances vary from culture to culture.

93

A day at a time

Many Africans take life one day at a time. The same applies to business. In Africa, planning your day in advance is a pretty futile exercise , because you can be assured that things will run a different course than you planned. The tax inspector may show up with a hefty assessment. A government authority may call you and threaten to close down your factory. A new decree may be announced. Some or all of your staff may not turn up. Everything may be completely different from the day before. That's simply a cultural 'given'.

So if you (at headquarters) want a particular report to be delivered to you by a certain date, say in three weeks' time, make sure you constantly remind the author over and over again about the deadline. If you don't, my bet is that you won't get anything. The author will simply think that, since you never mentioned it again, you no longer need the report.

Clearly, this is all about long-term v. short-term orientation.

Showing success

I know people in the Netherlands who have hidden their new Jaguar from their relatives and take their old Volkswagen to family events so as not to cause an upset. You're not supposed to flaunt your success here in our austere, Calvinist country as that is considered bragging. In the US, on the other hand, success is something to be proud of and something that other people, including your relatives, will congratulate you on.

This is a clear case of high masculinity in the US and low masculinity in the Netherlands. The Dutch apparently prefer to display their masculinity in other ways.

Giving instructions to a Dutchman

In the Netherlands, if you instruct or ask a subordinate to do something for you, you'd better explain why you need it (unless it's obvious). Give him or her some context. Don't be surprised if the subordinate challenges you if he or she thinks that what you're asking doesn't make sense. After you pass these 'tests', you'll get the job perfectly done. To manage Dutch people, you need to know what you're talking about and you need to be respected and supported to be effective.

Although an instruction given without any explanation or 'because I'm the boss' will probably get done, the employee performing it will lose every interest in doing a good job. Blind obedience is not a Dutch trait.

This is all about power distance and masculinity; the Dutch resent power and status.

Everyone takes pride in their job
In Africa, if you're accompanied by a driver and he offers to carry your briefcase, let him do it. The same applies if a porter wants to open the door for you. Don't rush, give him the time to get to his feet and let him open the door. It's his job, and he takes pride in doing it.

As I said, Africa scores very high on power distance.

15.4   The take-away

The first message here is be aware of the fact that the same behaviour can trigger entirely opposite reactions, depending on the culture you're dealing with. Being aware is halfway to winning the battle.

Secondly, prepare yourself before interacting with another culture. The differences can be immense. Culture is much more than how people hold their knife and fork when they eat or how they greet you. It is also about the sort of humour people like or resent, or the meaning of a handshake in business. A handshake in business can put you entirely on the wrong foot depending on where you are.

In short, be aware and be prepared.

16 The 'four types of employee' rule

16.1 The four types

As you know by now, I like to keep things simple. Well, this is a rule that really boils things down to the essence: *there are just four types of employees and this is how you deal with them.* I didn't come up with this one by myself, but I love it. A dear friend and former colleague told me about it. He might have heard it from someone like Jack Welsh[19], I don't know. It's so good, it could have been one of his. Here it is.

You can measure every employee by two criteria:
- does he or she deliver?
- does he or she display the right type of behaviour?

This makes four possible combinations:

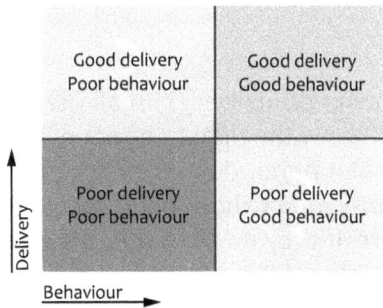

16.2 Now the rule

Everyone understands that people who don't display the right behaviour and don't deliver the goods should be sacked. And people who deliver the goods and show the right behaviour should be kept and cherished. So far, so good. You don't need a

---

[19] GE Chairman, 1981-2001.

97

rule for that.

The more complicated question is: how do you deal with people who do *deliver*, but display the *wrong behaviour* or people who *don't deliver* but do show the *right behaviour*?

Let's deal with the last category first. Just to be clear, the term 'right behaviour' refers to staff who are open, honest, don't hide their mistakes, don't blame others and help their colleagues out. These are people who are bright, eager to learn, work hard and who put their hands up if something needs to be done. That's the right behaviour!

Now the rule. If these well-behaved people don't deliver the goods, they should be coached, sent on courses and given another chances. Perhaps even two or three chances. You have to invest in them. If they still don't deliver, you'll then have to let them go. In that case, it's possible that your initial assessment was wrong to begin with.

But what about the people who do deliver (in mafia terms: the 'big earners'), but who don't show the right behaviour? They cheat, hide their mistakes, act like prima donnas, follow their own rules, overstep their authority, don't show any respect and set the wrong example to others. If they do all of this, it's easy. You fire them. But what if they only exhibit one or two of these symptoms? What do you do then? Still get rid of them, is the answer. And sooner rather than later. It may cost you in the short term, in profits and even in redundancy payments, but please go ahead and fire them. They'll cost you even more in the long run.

16.3   You want examples?

Think about your own experience. Every seasoned manager

has dealt with people like this. They're the sort of people who exceed their targets, always have an answer to any question, work very independently and need hardly any attention from the managing board. Sounds like the perfect employee, right? Wrong!

Let's say that you find out by sheer chance that they didn't follow company policy in a particular situation. They overstepped their authority. Then you start digging a bit deeper and find they dodged certain embargo rules. Then you hear how they cleverly bent local tax laws. When you ask them to account for themselves, they always have an explanation up their sleeve. It's always a 'plausible' explanation or excuse. Or they may claim that it was cleared by a superior who isn't there any more to confirm it (of course). Or they'll 'try to look up the e-mail later'.

These are the type of people who wouldn't surprise you if they did all sorts of deals on the side with their long-time business connections. Nevertheless, they still post a decent margin for you and meet their targets. You don't really trust them, but you just can't put your finger on why.

I think you're getting the idea. If you have a hunch like this, follow your gut feeling: fire him !

I had a business unit manager exactly like that. I learned the hard way. We tried to sell his business unit. He even brought in one of the prospective buyers. As we prepared for the buyer's due diligence, things began to unravel. We found that the manager in question had entered into commitments with one of his oldest and biggest customers that were far beyond his remit, were not in the company's interests and now completely destroyed the value of the business. Determined as we were to sell, and to not jeopardize the deal, we kept him on board and managed to sell him together with the business. We had to throw money at the deal to get it closed, but at least we got rid of him. With hindsight, we should have adhered to the 'four types of people rule' much earlier and should have sacked him years before. Believe me, the signals were there.

In another case, we *did* stick to the rule. This involved a guy who had just brought in a major new contract and reckoned he was now king of the castle. The company in question was almost bust, financially and organisationally, had just had a managing board shake-up and was going through a period of radical change. The board members were still very much in the process of communicating all the changes and convincing and motivating the business managers and other staff.

This particular manager agreed that things needed to change, but not in his vicinity. He knew everything better, sabotaged every change made by new board members, and decided on his own working hours. Nobody ever knew where he was or what he was doing. In fact, he was constantly challenging the authority of new board members. Clearly, it was the kind of behaviour you can do without. However, in most countries, and certainly in the Netherlands, such behaviour does not constitute sufficient grounds for dismissal.

The great thing with people like this, though, is that they tend to be predictable. So we looked into his expense claims and, bingo! There were claims for dinners and other forms of entertainment in his home town that had nothing to do with work. There were books and other personal items bought at airports on business trips and charged to his company account, fuel expense claims that were way out of line with his company car usage, etc.

And so we fired him on the spot, sending a number of clear messages to staff throughout the company. Perhaps the least important of these was that the company policy on expense claims was going to be strictly enforced once again from now on.

17 Technical developments and new tools, but how about planning?

17.1 Progress

I know that I sound like an old fogey when I tell you that, when I first started working, photocopiers were virtually a novelty. Back in those days, we had a copying machine with a rubber flap on top that used some kind of wet copying process. We had to feed in our documents page by page. At the time, most spreadsheets were handwritten and electronic spreadsheets ran on mainframes.

Since then, of course we have seen the development of fax machines, automatic colour copiers and printers, desktop PCs, laptop computers, Microsoft Office, voicemail, email, mobile phones, internet, SatNav, smart phones and now social media. Isn't it great? They all make life so much easier. Don't they?

All these tools are a tremendous help in our day-to-day work. It is impossible to imagine how we would do without them, and how in the past we actually did.

Without them, we would be lost. Every single deliverable would be late, every calculation would contain errors, and we would exchange written memos on paper (typed out by a secretary) and wait two days for a written reply (provided it came from the same office, that is). Every outgoing letter would be dictated to a secretary and then typed out by her. We would have to go to a library to do any kind of research. We would take hours and perhaps even days to find people and get hold of them on the phone.

It is just incredible how much progress has been made in business efficiency over the past 30 years.

17.2   Raising the bar

The only annoying thing about all this is that our peers and competitors have made exactly the same progress. All we have done is to raise the bar, time and time again, for ourselves and for others.

And so it is that, nowadays, everyone expects to receive an answer to a query within an hour. Similarly, people expect glossy PowerPoint presentations on any issue and comprehensive business cases supported by detailed calculations for every decision. And just about everyone who reckons he has something interesting to say can write and publish a management book.

Family life, weekends, holidays: nothing is sacred. Everyone has to be reachable at all times, no matter where they are or what they are doing. The only time you're excused for not responding instantly to an e-mail is when you're flying or in the loo. But you can't fight progress. After all, we all prosper and benefit from it.

17.3   Changing skills

There is only one thing you have got to remember and that is that all these tools also change the *skill* set that people develop.

When electronic calculators and automatic cash registers were first introduced, shop assistants soon lost the ability to calculate off the top of their head. They could no longer perform even the simplest computation without a machine.

Now, the same thing is happening to map-reading, the skill of finding your way around with the aid of a map. Many people have no idea of where they're driving and lose all sense of direction, simply because they're used to following a SatNav system. It's like being driven around in a strange city by a taxi, without a map to guide you. Even if you do it for weeks on end, you'll still have no idea of where you're going.

All this is perfectly okay for most jobs. The tool surely more than makes up for any lack of skill.

17.4   Planning, planning and more planning

The thing that worries me more, though, is the fact that people are starting to lose another, more important skill: *the ability to plan and to think ahead.* In business, almost everything hinges on planning and execution (or at least it should!). Proper planning is of paramount importance in running a company. Planning is key to getting things right first time. As Dwight D. Eisenhower said, 'a plan is nothing, but planning is everything!'

Nowadays, everybody can reach everyone else at any time. So why plan ahead? After all, you can just call your Mum from a train and ask her when to pick you up at the station.

Why plan a business trip, or your working day for that matter, in advance? You just e-mail your subordinate in the morning with a question that just came up, or that someone else asked you, and you can expect to receive a reply within the hour. If you *do* plan your day ahead, you can usually throw your plan out of the window as soon as you open your inbox in the morning anyway. One hundred incoming e-mails a day is no exception for today's on-line manager. Just reading them takes hours. Answering some of them may involve some actual work. After which the next pile lies waiting to be answered. Gone is your day, gone are your plans.

So my messages here are:
- Running a company also means planning, planning and planning.
- Be aware of the fact that people are losing their planning skills; be ready to train your staff.
- E-mail is the best tool of all, but the threshold is so low that it can easily become counterproductive. Be aware of this and introduce e-mail etiquette: reduce the number of e-mails, place limits on the number of people copied in to e-mails, the number and size of attachments, etc. Some people have already got into the habit of not opening their inbox during the morning – and telling their colleagues about this – so that they can at least set aside part of the day for themselves and get some work done. I'm convinced this type of behaviour will become more common over the next couple of years.

18   Value versus price

18.1   Mixing the two can be lethal

This is another stand-alone topic that is not necessarily relevant to everyone, but vitally important for many. It's critical to get it right. In the mergers and acquisition arena, mixing up value and price can be lethal. Believe me, I have seen my share of bloodshed.

Just bear the following in mind: you can *calculate* the value (of a business), but the *market* sets the price. These are two very different things, and the difference between them is not just semantics, as some people think. I'll explain why.

18.2   Discounted cash flow combined with sensitivity analysis

The value of a business is generally calculated by projecting future cash flows and residual value and discounting these to today with the aid of something known as the WACC[20].The result is the discounted cash flow value (DCF).

It's not worth going into detail here in order to explain how these cash flows are projected and how the WACC is determined. The principle should be self-explanatory.

Projecting cash flows has its inherent flaws. Predicting the future is not an exact science. There will be margins of error and

---

[20] Weighted average cost of capital.

there will be uncertainties, especially if the business is not mature yet. For this reason, a proper DCF valuation should always go hand in hand with a sensitivity analysis (and with historic figures and trends, if possible). A sensitivity analysis will show how changes in your basic assumptions affect the DCF value. The historic figures and trends will increase your comfort, but are only meaningful in relation to relatively mature businesses. They're all very useful to get a good feel of how robust the valuation is.

As I said, DCF valuation has its drawbacks. However, it is undeniably superior to any other valuation method. When used in combination with a sensitivity analysis, it is by far the best way of valuing a business. It forms the basis for all business valuations. Or at least it should.

afloat

val·ley [val-ee] n
or hollow,
wave.
val·ue [
something in term
amount of other
which it can be ex
of some

18.3   Using multiples

The other method often used for valuations is one based on multiples, commonly of EBITA or another profit or cash flow ratio. Often, this method is still an indirect valuation based on the DCF. The 'multiple approach' is merely a shortcut, a way of jumping from a proper DCF valuation of one company to a quick, multiple-based valuation of another. Both companies need to be comparable, though, in terms of activities and growth rate.

It only gets tricky when companies are valued on the basis of multiples only and similar companies or similar transactions are used as benchmarks without going back to basics, i.e. the DCF. If you do this, you'll find that you've crossed the line between value and price and are in fact just looking at price.

18.4   The 'value' of an art painting

Let me explain it in another way. Facebook is currently 'valued' at some USD 50-60 billion. No one knows what this figure is based on, but this is what Goldman Sachs are telling us. So it must be true, right? Or are Goldman Sachs just telling us what the price is? And are they conveniently calling it the 'value'. I think so.

It's like an art auction house that tells you what the estimated price of a painting is. They estimate what they think the market will pay for it; they are the 'authority' providing the estimate. Of course, they also have an interest in a high price, as do Goldman Sachs, but let's ignore this factor for now. In the case of paintings, the estimate is bound to be based on the price of similar paintings by the same or a similar artist. Comparable deals, comparable prices. Let's be clear, though: this is all about price, not value. If you really want to know the *value* of a painting, you ought to look at the production cost, i.e. the cost of materials and time, plus a reasonable margin. Nobody would be interested in that, of course, but it would be a logical approach.

If you want to know the *value* of Facebook, let them tell you what exactly their business models are, what their projected proceeds and costs will be, what these were in the past and what the estimated long-term growth rates are. Then you can do a decent DCF valuation. Since all that information is not yet known, certainly not in detail, we can in fact only talk about 'price'.

18.5   Strategic or speculative?

Now back to buying businesses. If you're buying a business, you've got to ask yourself whether you're a *strategic* or a *speculative* buyer.

In most business acquisitions, the reason is of course strategic. In other words, you're buying in order to achieve synergies. So if you buy for strategic reasons, you've got to *value* the business and pay a price based on that valuation. Buyers often include part of the (potential) future synergy in the price that they are willing to pay. That's a choice, but do be very careful about this![21] Sometimes, buyers even include *all* future synergies in their price. In that case, it's hardly worth bothering. The best strategy is of course to pay a price below the value.

Now, if you're a speculative buyer and you think that you'll be able to sell something at a better *price* in the future than the price you're paying today, then you might be able to focus on price and forget about value. In that case, you can pay more than the value. But you've got to be pretty sure about the future.

This is precisely the game Goldman Sachs are playing with Facebook. Moreover, this is the game all merchant bankers were playing during the 'dot com' boom. If they didn't know exactly how to calculate the value of a business, they just looked at previous deals (also brokered by one of them), compared various multiples and drove the market into a frenzy. They were deal-pushers, nothing more. Their mantra was 'the market is always

---

[21] Numerous studies have demonstrated that the majority of acquisitions are failures, many for exactly this reason. See, for example, Straub, Thomas. *Reasons for frequent failure in mergers and acquisitions – a comprehensive analysis*, Deutscher Universitätsverlag, Wiesbaden, 2007.

right and price equals value'. So, cheered and advised by their merchant bankers, companies started buying businesses, or licenses as the case may be, based on *price* instead of *value*. The rest is history.

Again, buying on price is wise only if you're speculating and reckon you know how the price is going to develop in the future. But never buy on price if you're buying for strategic reasons!

So why does everyone still look at value calculations, even if they are just speculating on the stock market? The answer is simple: because *value* is always the best support for a *price*. It may not be for a work of art, but it is for a business.

19   The human factor

You may have noticed that the 'human factor' is a recurring theme in this book. It's no coincidence. An organisation is nothing more than a bunch of people working together to deliver a service or product. So the better you align your people – both with each other and with the other stakeholders' interests – the better your company will perform.

Elsewhere in this book you've read about delegation, empowerment, the four types of employee, cultural differences, leadership, leading by example, allowing people to make mistakes, listening to people and identifying and coaching talented staff. These are all vital ingredients – must-haves – for an excellent company. However, there is a bit more to say about 'human capital'.

Firstly, remember that employees are more than just a resource. They're not comparable with machines and financial resources. Unfortunately for some, staff think and feel. That means that they may get unhappy and frustrated and hence may lose their motivation to perform for the company. Some businesses are clearly more sensitive to this than others, but generally, happy, motivated and proud employees are a huge asset to any company and a prerequisite for success. This dimension doesn't come into play with other resources.

So you've got to keep your staff happy and motivated and reward them properly (within reason, of course). Take them seriously, listen to them, give them career prospects and inform them. Sometimes, you may want to give them more information than is strictly required. They'll pay you back in loyalty. They'll go the extra mile for you and for the company, and they'll try to solve problems instead of dumping them on your desk at 5 pm. Unhappy staff can become a liability to a company. Replacing them is costly and takes up a lot of management time. So try and avoid it.

However, if people are being unreasonable, apply the 'four types of employee' rule and act accordingly. Simple.

Secondly, and I may be stating the obvious, but in order to run an excellent company, you got to have all your 'human resource bases' covered:

- a proper and transparent pay system, with clear prospects for everyone;
- a system of periodical appraisals based on targets that, at least in part, tie in with the annual plan and budgets;
- a policy on the ratio between the fixed and variable components of pay; the variable component should be tied into the appraisal system (i.e. linked to the annual plan and budget);
- an overall package of pay and fringe benefits that corresponds more or less with current market practice;
- a management development programme for talented young staff.

It's imperative that you put all this in place. In effect, they close the 'running a company' circle. They provide you with a mechanism to incentivise people to do the right things and let them share in their, and your, success. You can't run a company on goodwill alone.

20　This is how you do it

- Obey the four basic principles
- Stick to the seven ground rules for effective behaviour
- Be aware of cultural differences within your organisation
- Plan whatever you do and plan properly
- Empower your staff – the right person in the right place – and push responsibilities down as far as you can
- Keep your HQ as small as possible
- Let HQ focus on setting and controlling the framework and creating the right conditions for the operating units
- Set up and plan a proper review and control process
- Make synergy the leading theme in structuring your company and in your strategic moves
- Avoid ambiguity; embrace transparency and consistency
- Avoid complexity in structure, reporting, processes and systems.
- Don't chase perfection, be effective
- Acknowledge the human factor and tie your people into the success of the company
- Above all: KEEP THINGS SIMPLE!

About the author

Wim Kromhout, a Dutch national, has over 30 years' experience in managing people and businesses in a wide range of industries. His career roots are in public accounting in the Netherlands and the United States with one of the big six accounting firms, where he found himself managing its biggest Dutch audit client in the early nineties and was poised to become an audit partner in 1995.

He then made a career change and joined one of the largest public companies in the Netherlands, the incumbent telecom operator, where he soon headed up the Strategic Control Department.

This allowed him to be very close to the Board and decision-making processes at a time when the telephony industry was going through a period of unprecedented turbulence. The growth of mobile telephony, cable television and the internet and other IT services, against the backdrop of privatisations and ever-changing regulations, paired with a changing management morale, made this without doubt one of the most dynamic times in modern business.

Since then, Wim Kromhout has held various posts as a CFO, in international telephony, the rapidly growing then collapsing internet industry, and an aviation company that needed to be restructured in the wake of 9/11.

In 2005, he started his own consultancy. His most significant assignment was to financially lead a multi-billion-pound PFI bid in the United Kingdom.

Wim Kromhout never planned his career. With hindsight, it feels like he couldn't have planned it better:

- a 17-year foundation of international public accounting in the Netherlands and the USA, interrupted by 16 months as a cadet in the Dutch army,
- over five years with one of the largest publicly listed companies in the Netherlands, during an extremely turbulent period,
- 1½ years with an extremely fast-growing internet start-up,
- five years with a 60-year-old legacy company that needed to reorganise, and reorganise dramatically, in order to survive,
- advising on mergers & acquisitions and corporate restructuring, and financially leading a multi-billion pound bid in the City.

If you wonder why you have never come across a lecture or article by Wim Kromhout before, the answer is simple: he was far too busy doing all the above and hadn't yet learned how to go home at a decent time of day.

With many thanks to my 'pre-readers':
Jan Buné, David Rae,
Ronald van Rossum and Paul Verheul

Language editor:
Tony Parr

Layout, cover and illustrations:
Nanny van den Boogaart

Graphics:
Margot Kromhout (yes, my daughter)

www.ingramcontent.com/pod-product-compliance
Lightning Source LLC
Chambersburg PA
CBHW060619210326
41520CB00010B/1399